IMAGES
of America

THROGGS NECK
PELHAM BAY

The Bayard farm of the early 1800s stood at the lower end of Pelham Bay Park, north of Middletown Road. It later became the John Hunter III Estate called Anneswood. This tintype of the caretaker's family was taken in the 1800s.

IMAGES
of America

THROGGS NECK
PELHAM BAY

Bill Twomey and John McNamara

ARCADIA
PUBLISHING

Published by Arcadia Publishing
Charleston, South Carolina

Library of Congress Catalog Card Number: 98-88062

For all general information contact Arcadia Publishing at:
Telephone 843-853-2070
Fax 843-853-0044
E-mail sales@arcadiapublishing.com
For customer service and orders:
Toll-Free 1-888-313-2665

Visit us on the Internet at www.arcadiapublishing.com

*Dedicated to our parents, Frank and Catherine "Jerry"
Twomey, and John and Betty McNamara.*

CONTENTS

ACKNOWLEDGMENTS

This modest pictorial would not have been possible without the generosity of those who have shared their treasured photographs with us. It is hoped that this sharing will help preserve these pictures and the memories they invoke for future generations. Ron Schliessman has been a great help in providing numerous photographs as has the *Bronx Times Reporter*. The Chippewa Democratic Club, the Bronx County Historical Society, the Ralph Giordano Funeral Home, and the Throggs Neck Little League are also to be thanked. Gratitude is also extended to others who have offered or provided photographs or information including John V. Riche, Carol Gross, May Mastrarrigo, Tom Tarantino, Barbara Powers, Bill Zawar, Italo Mazzella, Frank Morea, Henry Westerman, A. Treanor, Wesley Boes, Paul Miller, Peter Macchia, the Scolaro and Slattery families, John Pye, John and Irma Gallagher, Jack McCarrick, Don Engeldrum, Kenneth Aitken, May Doherty, Marco D'Antonio, Charlie Maguire, Catherine Converso, the Twomey family, Anthony R. Ferrara, Earl Hansen, Lawrence Schliessman, Billy Goldsmith, George Finnin Sr., Elise Thomma, Ken Roberts, Michael McGrory, the Solfio family, and Edward Wolf.

INTRODUCTION

The title of this book, *Throggs Neck-Pelham Bay*, is meant to imply not only these two communities, but all the other neighborhoods in between. Together, they are encompassed within the boundaries of John Throckmorton's settlement of 1642. Called the Vriedlandt ("land of peace") by Dutch authorities, it was bounded on the west by Westchester Creek and its tributaries leading to the Hutchinson River, which forms the northern boundary where it flows into Eastchester Bay. Eastchester Bay in the Long Island Sound is the eastern boundary, and the East River is at the South.

The area had been home to the Siwanoy Indians, a sub-tribe of the Mohegans, both before and after Throckmorton. John Throckmorton, an Englishman, had emigrated with Roger Williams from Massachusetts to Rhode Island in 1637. His patent of the Vriedlandt is dated 1643, but he settled on the land with 35 families in 1642 while awaiting the actual document. His settlement was located on today's Schurz Avenue in the vicinity of Calhoun Avenue and was short-lived due to the Indian Wars of 1643. Although he returned to Rhode Island, Throckmorton did retain ownership of the land which bears his name, albeit in abridged form, to this very day. Throckmorton sold his land in the Vriedlandt to Augustine Hermans in 1652, and it has since been continually subdivided.

Thomas Pell of Fairfield, Connecticut purchased a large tract of land, including today's New Rochelle, Pelham, Pelham Manor, Eastchester, and parts of the Bronx from the Siwanoy Indians on November 14, 1654. The site of his purchase is located near the Bartow-Pell Mansion, and the tree under which the purchase was made was called Treaty Oak. The tree is long gone, but the site has been preserved with a wrought iron fence. The name of the Bronx community of Pelham Bay is a reminder of Thomas Pell and his descendants who were lords of the manor.

Although this work is limited to 128 pages, every effort has been made to provide a strong overview of the communities encompassed in the area with the photographs available to the authors.

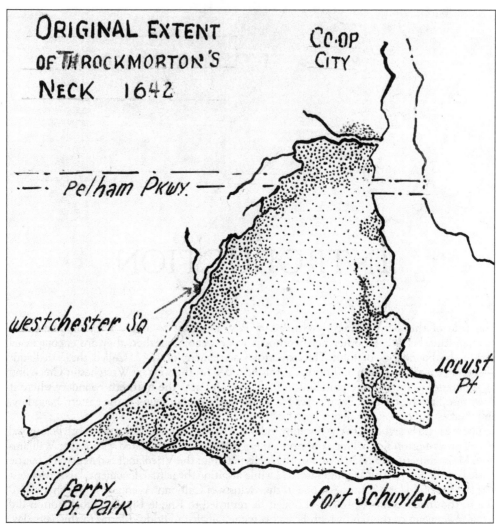

Using 21st-century placenames, Westchester Creek is at the tip of Ferry Point and forms the water boundary, northeasterly, almost to Co-op City. At the Hutchinson River (upper right) the boundary turns south through Eastchester Bay, rounds Fort Schuyler into the East River, and ends at Ferry Point.

One

CHURCHES AND CLERGY

The Ralph Giordano Funeral Home provided this photograph of what appears to be the Poscillico funeral on the steps of St. Theresa's old church. It was taken in the early 1930s, and the gate of heaven adornment at the left was borne through the streets as part of this grand funeral procession led by the latest Pierce-Arrows.

The facade of the Fort Schuyler Presbyterian Church on Dewey Avenue between Edison and Logan Avenues has changed over the years, and this photograph should be a pleasant reminder of a quiet and simpler time.

The Fort Schuyler Presbyterian Church choir was performing on Dewey Avenue in this 1955 photograph. PS 72 would be across the street to the left.

Ron Schliessman took this photograph of the old wooden St. Benedict's church in February of 1956. He was looking southeast from Edison Avenue and Bruckner Boulevard.

Msgr. Robert A. Brucato (right) is seen here being installed as pastor of St. Benedict's Church by Msgr. Henry Vier on November 22, 1987.

11

The Hellenic Orthodox Community on Bruckner Boulevard was constructing their grand church when this photograph was taken from Willow Lane.

The Ladies' Auxiliary of the Schneider-Sampson Veterans of Foreign Wars Post stand by a barn on Barkley Avenue, west and down the hill from the 45th precinct. The earliest services of the First Lutheran Church of Throggs Neck, now on Baisley Avenue, were held here.

Crow Hill is a two-century-old name for the slope opposite today's Lehman High School. Not quite as old is the First Presbyterian Church of Throggs Neck atop the hill since 1855. During the Civil War, it was called "the Soup Church" by soldiers passing through. Parishioners would meet them at the train station and offer them a bowl of soup to keep them from the taverns. About a decade later, the church burned down and was rebuilt in stone. It was restored in the 1980s.

Rev. Richard Bortle Mattice
(1850–1922) served as pastor of
the First Presbyterian Church of
Throggs Neck for 32 years prior
to his retirement in 1920.

Ed Schmidt is examining some of
the historic monuments at the First
Presbyterian Church of Throggs Neck
on Crow Hill at East Tremont Avenue
and Ericson Place.

14

Msgr. Fulton J. Sheen (1895–1979) was the host of the "Catholic Hour" on NBC radio when this picture was taken in 1930. He was already recognized as an orator of note and was speaking at the dedication of St. Frances de Chantal Church and School. Years later, in 1951, he started his television broadcast, "Life is Worth Living."

The St. Frances de Chantal Church and School dedication took place in May of 1930. Note the attire of the children. The girls are all wearing bonnets, and the younger boys have short pants on while the older ones are sporting "knickers."

Monsignor Lavelle participated in the 1930 dedication of St. Frances de Chantal Church and School. The first pastor was Father William Jordan.

This is a photograph of the entourage leaving the rectory for the dedication ceremonies of St. Frances de Chantal Church and School.

Matty Pueraro has his hands on the two shovels used in this groundbreaking ceremony for St. Frances de Chantal Church on Hollywood Avenue in 1969. Matty was born in the town of Torrito, in Bari, Italy and eventually settled in Throggs Neck where he became very active in both the parish and the community. He is predominant in this picture because of his service and dedication to the church. The man with the eyeglasses to his right is Joe Caggiano, also active in the parish. A smiling Msgr. John T. Halpin, the pastor, is seen between them.

Jack McCarrick took this photograph of the dedication of Msgr. John T. Halpin Place on January 8, 1984. From left to right are: Jack Lynch, Kathleen Lynch, Msgr. Joseph Devlin, John Ferrick, and John McNamara. Jack was standing on Hollywood Avenue facing Msgr. Halpin Place, which was formerly called Silver Beach Place.

New street signs were installed on the former Silver Beach Place noting the name change to Msgr. John T. Halpin Place on January 8, 1984. Councilman Michael DeMarco poses with the monsignor in this photograph. Sister Mary Stanislaus is in the center.

Two

Schools and Students

Preston High School was established in 1947 by the Sisters of Divine Compassion at the Schurz Avenue mansion that was once home to railroad tycoon Collis P. Huntington. Mother Mary Aloysia Kelly was the founding principal, and the school was named in honor of Msgr. Thomas Preston, who co-founded the Sisters of Divine Compassion. The school graduated its first class in 1951, and Barbara Powers provided this photograph of the 1952 graduates. Sister Lucille Coldrick is the current principal.

The little wooden schoolhouse pictured here was the original PS 14. It was built in 1857 as District School 3 and had only one room. Additions were made in 1873 and 1879, and in 1895, when this area was ceded to New York City by Westchester County, it became known as PS 99. Shortly thereafter, the schools were renumbered, and it became PS 14. Another addition was made in 1905, and the building remained in use until the current brick building was opened on September 10, 1928. This building, as the sign indicates, became an annex to James Monroe High School.

Norma Carbone provided this picture of her fifth grade class at PS 14. Taken over 50 years ago, Mrs. J. Wolski was the teacher, and the students included Margaret Amoroso, Anthony Blancato, Norma Boz, John Cali, Lucy DeAngelo, Joseph DeLucia, Ronald Feliciano, Nicholas Filannino, Angie Fogliazzia, Anna Finnerty, Jean Gowers, Lucille Ippilito, Richard Lawson, William Lorusso, Antoinette Mennitti, Rosalie Mennitti, Robert Morehead, Tina Rotanelli, Filomena Stingone, Stanley Sokalski, Antoinette Wisich, Marjorie Wright, Marie Paccione, Joseph Carlini, Joseph Ellsworth, Roy Rosenberg, Robert Melville, Thomas Annunziata, Edward Schaefer, Balbo Esposito, Raymond Schmitt, Thomas Kelly, Gerard DiMelfi, Frances Raineri ,and Rosemarie Mirando.

Youngsters attending PS 14 participated in a dance fest in this photograph. The A & P and St. Benedict's Church are in the background.

Ron Schliessman took this photograph showing the northeast corner of Crosby Avenue and Bruckner Boulevard on December 10, 1956 before the expressway was constructed. The large brick building is PS 14.

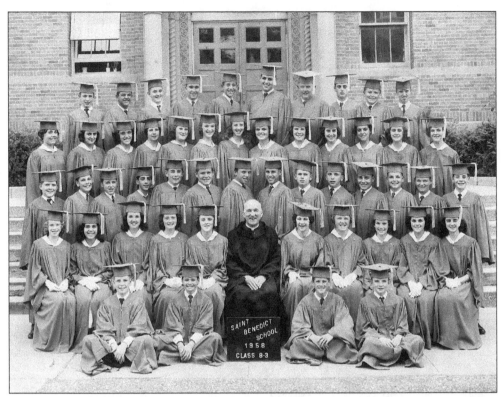

The 1958 graduation class of St. Benedict School posed with Father Albert, the pastor, in this photograph supplied by Dennis Rosa.

Police Officer Edward R. Byrne was honored posthumously when Henry Bruckner Junior High School 101 on Lafayette Avenue was renamed for him in April of 1989. His uniform was put on display for the occasion.

KINNERSLEY SC.　　　　　　　　　　　　　　　　J. W. HARRISON, PRINTER.

WEST CHESTER BOARDING-SCHOOL,
BY ELLWOOD WALTER.

This Institution is exclusively for boys, and is located in the Village of West Chester, about 12 miles from the City of New-York, on the mail road to New-Haven. The situation is pleasant, and probably, as healthy as any in the state.

There is a daily mail to and from the city, and communication, by Stage, with the Harlæm Railroad, twice a day.

The usual branches of an English education, Mathematics, and the Greek, Latin and French languages are embraced in the course of instruction, which will be carefully pursued with a view to prepare the pupil for entering College, or for engaging in Mercantile business.

Familiar lectures on Chemistry, Natural Philosophy and Astronomy, illustrated by apparatus, and designed to interest scholars in the study of these Sciences, will be delivered, in connection with the recitation of lessons from approved text books.

The School, Dining and Lodging Rooms are so arranged as to afford facilities for a constant supervision of the pupils.

There is ample space in the Play-ground for exercise and amusement, and a large room is appropriated to these purposes in inclement weather.

There are two Vacations in the course of the year; one during the last two weeks of Fifth Month, (May) and the other, the first two weeks of Tenth Month, (Oct.)

Pupils are required to furnish their own beds and bedding. All articles of bedding and clothing should be distinctly marked with the owner's name or initials.

TERMS.

For board, with tuition in the English branches only, $45; with the languages, or Mathematics, included, $50 per quarter, payable in advance.

The quarter consists of 12 weeks. No extra charges for Washing, Mending or Stationery.

REFERENCES in the City of New-York :

CORNELIUS W. LAWRENCE,	ROBERT I. WALKER,	JOHN D. WRIGHT,
SAUL ALLEY,	WM. L. ROFF,	HENRY HAYDOCK,
RAMSAY CROOKS,	MULFORD MARTIN,	DAVID LUDLAM, JR
WALTER B. TOWNSEND,	HENRY H. BARROW,	ROBERT M. STRATTON
WILLIAM WILLIS,	WILLIAM ADEE,	THOMAS HAZARD,
JOSIAH MACY,	FREDERICK A. TALLMADGE,	E. K. COLLINS

THIRD MONTH, 1842

In 1842, this broadside advertised an exclusive boarding school for boys that was located in Westchester Village on the Westchester Turnpike, but the school was soon relocated to Crow Hill, now bisected by Dudley and Coddington Avenues. It later became a roadhouse.

A rainy day on Westchester Avenue couldn't dampen the spirits of the Rose E. Scala School girls. Also known as PS 71, the school has served the area since 1927.

Getting ready for a parade has these girls of St. Theresa in a good mood. The street behind them now bears the name of the church and school but had been Morris Park Avenue until 1968.

Our Lady of Assumption School was once located on Kearney Avenue off Country Club Road. Father John McCahill had purchased the old mansion, c. 1928, and the school was established under the care of the Dominican nuns.

Tom Tarantino supplied these snapshots of Our Lady of Assumption School taken in 1954 shortly before the school moved to Middletown Road.

The St. Joseph's Way dedication ceremonies for the naming of the roadway to St. Joseph's School for the Deaf took place on March 18, 1988. The school is one of the leading educational facilities in the borough.

Although Villa Maria Academy has plenty of trees around it, Arbor Day was still observed when this picture was snapped at the beautiful school on Country Club Road. The 112-year-old school has occupied the former Ellis Estate for the past 70 years.

PS 72 at Edison and Dewey Avenues looks extremely modern in contrast to its rural setting in 1929.

The thespians pictured here were attending PS 72 when this picture was taken, c. 1925. Dewey Avenue is at right, and the photographer was looking east.

Students and staff take part in the planting of a tree during this Arbor Day ceremony at PS 72, c. 1929.

The construction of Fort Schuyler took place between 1833 and 1856, and the name honored Gen. Philip Schuyler, who commanded the Northern Army in 1777. The lighthouse keeper, "Captain" Charles Ferreira, has just welcomed fifth graders from PS 72 in the year 1929. The grounds are now home to the New York State Maritime Academy.

The St. Frances de Chantal elementary school unfurled their "Great Quilt" on March 28, 1976. It measured 30 by 24 feet and contained 1,200 panels created by the students. It was reputed to be the largest quilt in the world, and Congressman Mario Biaggi was on hand to attest to its dimensions.

Sister Mary Bernard, R.D.C., became the first principal of St. Frances de Chantal School when it opened on September 8, 1930. While serving as principal, she also taught the eighth grade.

Students line the stairs in this photograph of the unveiling of the "Great Quilt" at St. Frances.

Sister Mary Callista, R.D.C., and Sister Mary Bertrand, R.D.C., of St. Frances de Chantal School, pose in modified habits.

Robert Barrett was the longtime principal of I.S. 192 and is accepting an award on behalf of his school in this photograph.

This photograph of Pauline Ungerer was taken in 1928 and shows the typical attire of an eighth grade graduate of our public school system.

Three

MANSIONS, ESTATES, AND FARMS

In Civil War times, this was the Fox Mansion of Pennyfield, which became known in the 1930s to 1960s as "Charley's Mansion" near Miles Avenue. A fire destroyed it in May 1963, and an apartment house took its place.

This stone mansion in Edgewater Park harks back to 1853 when a family named Adee had it built. The building had 11 rooms until 1860 when nine more were added, and local folklore has it that Mrs. Adee was the one who named the estate Edgewater. In 1910, an Irishman, Richard Shaw, leased the land for a stock farm and lived in the mansion with his family. He allowed the St. Ann's Cadets to bivouac on a meadow and practice marching, gunnery, and swimming. Some parents would also ask permission to tent there on weekends. Gradually, others came and put up tents. These seasonal campers eventually erected wooden bungalows, and a well next to the mansion became inadequate for the growing population, so pipes led to community faucets and outhouses. Electricity followed. The Shaw family eventually formed a corporation and bought the property from the Adee sons. Edgewater Park has since become a co-op.

John Hunter III sold this mansion and property north of Middletown Road to the Parks Department in 1888. Later, it was Kane's Casino of Pelham Bay Park. The Sunday visitor in 1936 was Gus Wehr, a former German seaman.

In 1893, Emily Potter purchased a tract of land with its magnificent view of Eastchester Bay from the Westchester Land Corporation. The mansion and grounds were a showplace that later became Providence Rest Nursing Home. It is located at Waterbury and Stadium Avenues.

The Abijah Hammond Mansion was built c. 1805 when the area was owned by a Revolutionary War colonel. It was considerably improved in the late 1890s by Theodore Havemeyer, then the owner, and is still a landmark. It is located in Silver Beach and houses their administrative offices.

This photograph of the same mansion was taken in 1993, 72 years after the one above.

This 40-room mansion on Sampson Avenue between Revere and Calhoun Avenues was built in 1870 for John A. Morris, who financed the Morris Park Racecourse in 1888. The last owner, in 1921, was Najeeb Kiamie, a wealthy Lebanese merchant who soundproofed some of the rooms so that his wife, three sons, and a daughter could find quiet havens in their home. It was razed *c.* 1945.

This photograph of the Van Schaick mansion at Schurz and East Tremont Avenues was taken in 1928, several years before it was razed. Peter Van Schaick left the money to build the free reading room at Westchester Square. The town could not accept the gift, however, due to the high cost of maintaining the building. Collis P. Huntington provided these funds, and today the free library bears his name.

The Coster family traced their ancestry back to the Dutch period of Nieuw Amsterdam and, in the 19th century, had a thriving fruit nursery. It extended from today's Lafayette Avenue to Bruckner Boulevard and from East Tremont Avenue to the Throgs Neck Expressway. Their mansion was built around 1838 at Edison Avenue and Greene Place, and, when it was razed, St. Benedict's School took its place.

The Brinsmade Estate once stretched from the Fort Road (East Tremont Avenue) west to Baxter's Creek (the cemetery) and from Dill Place north to Barkley Avenue. The mansion had to be moved 50 yards south when Lafayette Avenue was cut through. The structure was damaged by the move, and the Swedish Lutheran Society's Home for the Aged gave up its tenancy in 1964.

Opposite the Pelham Golf Course can be found the Bartow-Pell Mansion. The 200-acre estate was acquired by Robert Bartow in 1836, and he moved into the mansion in 1842. His family resided there until 1888, after which the house fell into disrepair and was eventually taken over by the City of New York for various uses. The International Garden Club took it over in 1914 and have since made a show place out of it. The site of "Treaty Oak" is fenced off and may be seen off to the right when entering the estate. This is the site where Thomas Pell is said to have purchased 9,000 acres of land from the Siwanoy in 1654. The tree was destroyed by a bolt of lightning in 1906, and only the fenced-in site remains to mark the spot.

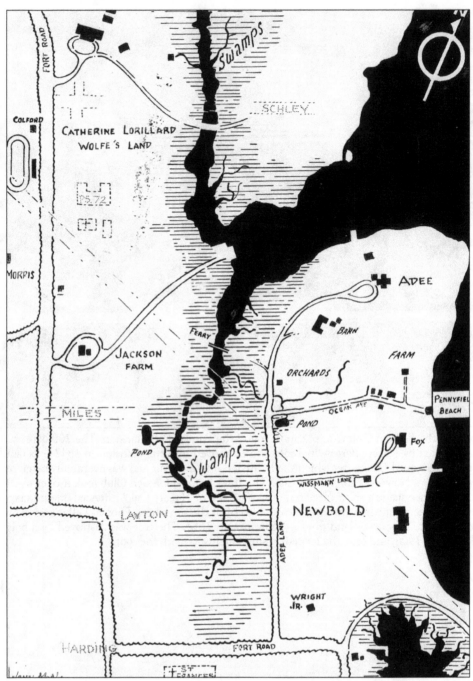

This map is a composite of several old-timers' memories of 1890. On the north is Randall Avenue, east is Long Island Sound, Harding Avenue marks the south, and East Tremont Avenue is on the west. The Adee Estate is now Edgewater Park, and Adee Lane is Meagher Avenue. Colford Oval was south of Schley Avenue, and the Jackson farm is covered by Engine 72 Ladder. Newbold's land touched Wissman and Harding Avenues. Ocean Avenue is now Miles Avenue and led to Pennyfield Beach. The Wolfe Estate ran from Randall Avenue south to PS 72 and the First Presbyterian Church of Throggs Neck.

When this picture was taken in the 1880s, Locust Point was an island and had only one home, seen here at left. The occupants of this home were Capt. George Wright and his family. The house was located at approximately 177th Street and Glennon Place, and the island was known as Wright's Island. This view is to the northeast.

In 1890, Capt. George Wright's coach house, hay and stock barns, and sheep pen stood where the Throgs Neck Bridge toll booths are located. Wright's Island is now called Locust Point, and the sheep are long gone.

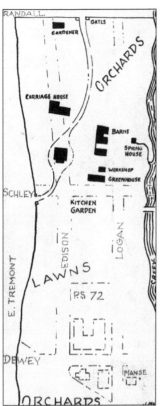

The Doric Farm of the Wolfe family (1830–1895), in today's terms, was approximately bounded by Randall, East Tremont, and Sampson Avenues. Weir Creek is at the right and has since been covered by the Throgs Neck Expressway.

The pillared entrance to Catherine Lorillard Wolfe's estate met the Fort Road (now East Tremont Avenue) at approximately Schley Avenue. This view, c. 1900, is to the south.

The Doric Mansion was named for the Doric columns of John D. Wolfe's home in 1830. Wolfe's daughter, Catherine Lorillard Wolfe, sold the property around 1895, and the mansion was razed in 1929 to make room for Edison Avenue.

Folklore credits this house on Sunset Trail in Silver Beach as belonging to James Fenimore Cooper, of literary fame. Church records tell a different tale. James Cooper's brother, William Cooper, lived there long before it was razed around 1945.

JOHN S. MAPES, Auctioneer

Of H. C. MAPES & CO.

Office, 1469 WILLIAMSBRIDGE ROAD, N. Y. CITY

AUCTION SALE

214 CHOICE LOTS

KNOWN AS THE

KOCH HOMESTEAD

DESIRABLY SITUATED ON AND NEAR

MIDDLETOWN ROAD

DIRECTLY OPPOSITE TREMONT TERRACE. THREE BLOCKS EAST OF
WESTCHESTER AVENUE AS EXTENDED AND FIVE BLOCKS
WEST OF PELHAM PARK AT

WESTCHESTER

BRONX BOROUGH

Saturday, June 19, '09

AT 1 O'CLOCK

ON THE GROUNDS

RAIN OR SHINE ============ UNDER A TENT

SEND TO THE AUCTIONEER FOR MAPS

The broadside for the auction of the Koch homestead sets the date at Saturday, June 19, 1909.

Migrant workers on the Buhre, Baxter, Koch, and Cornell farms were of varied nationalities. Italians predominated, but there were numerous Irish and German farmhands, and some of them remained to buy land of their own and send for their families.

44

The location map for the Koch Homestead auction of 1909 shows only the Westchester Avenue trolley line since the subway had not yet reached Westchester Square. Note that Tremont Avenue was still called Fort Schuyler Road.

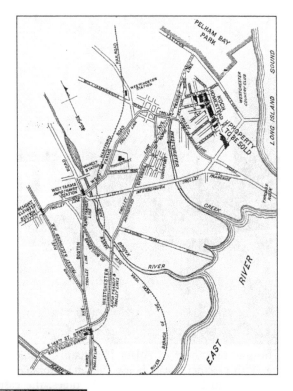

The Koch family had two farms from the 1890s to World War I. One tract ran from approximately Buhre Avenue south to Wellman Avenue, and the other included LaSalle Avenue south to Bruckner Boulevard (PS 14). Their farmhouse was at 1528 Plymouth Avenue, and the back porch in 1906 provided a rest for Frederick Koch (left) and his son of the same name.

The sole remainder of Adam Hoffmann's Picnic Grounds was the casino situated behind the 45th precinct stationhouse (at left). Hoffmann's grounds once extended from Bruckner Boulevard to Lafayette Avenue. At times, the casino had also been the Crosby Mansion and Capalbo's Inn.

Teresa and Adam Hoffmann are in their wedding garb in this 1895 photograph.

<table>
<tr><td>PIC --- NIC GROUNDS</td><td>TELEPHONE 246 WESTCHESTER</td><td>BASE-BALL GROUNDS</td></tr>
</table>

A. HOFFMANN'S
HOTEL AND PARK

EASTERN BOULEVARD AND
FORT SCHUYLER ROAD

THROGGS NECK, WESTCHESTER, N. Y. CITY 46

TWO **DANCE HALLS**	**DIRECTION:** END OF FORT SCHUYLER CAR LINE	**BOWLING** **ALLEYS**

Adam Hoffmann was a name often encountered in the early Bronx because the Bavarian immigrant had already learned the beer brewing trade in the old country. In 1913, Hoffmann's Park at today's Bruckner Boulevard and East Tremont Avenue was his most successful venture. There were ball games, clambakes, barbecues, turtle fests, harvest festivals, and merry-go-rounds. In 1919, at the peak of his career, Adam Hoffmann died and was buried in nearby St. Raymond's Cemetery.

Teresa (Reissner) was the second wife of Adam Hoffmann and bore him six children.

47

The Wissmann Mansion overlooked the Long Island Sound and later became a popular Viennese restaurant and dance hall known as the Vindabona with a clientele largely German and Austrian. After WW II, the building became the Open Fireplace and finally the Theodore Korony Post. It was razed in 1986.

Francis De Ruyter Wissmann owned an estate called Pennyfield. This 1870 photograph is of his father and brother, both named Frederick.

Francis Wissmann owned Pennyfield, an estate bounded by Harding, Meagher, and Wissman Avenues, east to the Long Island Sound. He was an abrasive squire, constantly embroiled in law suits and matters involving riparian rights; however, he should go down in local history for two reasons. First, he donated the meadow on which the first tent church of St. Frances de Chantal was established. Second, Longstreet Avenue was named in honor of a Confederate general upon his request.

The mansion of Francis Morris, built in the 1850s, was just as imposing almost a century later when Gene Zeumer, lower right, strolled by. In 1947, it was a German-American restaurant and dance hall with a stadium behind it called Throggs Neck Stadium. The prior name had been German Stadium.

In 1850, Francis Morris's 80-acre tract along the East River was enhanced by this mansion which was to be occupied by generations who added another 70 acres by 1922. The property was subdivided, and the Schurz Avenue's extension caused the partial razing of what had become German Stadium's fashionable restaurant. Dr. Brancati was the proprietor when this picture was taken, and Gene Zeumer obtained it later.

This house, located at the corner of Brinsmade and Lawton Avenues, was the gatehouse of the Morris Estate. It was razed in 1968 at which time it was approximately a century old. The photograph was taken in 1950.

Charlie Maguire took this photograph of the stone wall behind the former Archer Milton Huntington Estate in Pelham Bay Park. The Pelham Bay Landfill at Tallapoosa Point is in the background.

The horse cemetery beyond the police stables is located just east of the old Rice Stadium site on the former Archer Milton Huntington Estate. The cemetery is rediscovered every few years, and this picture was taken by Charlie Maguire.

The DiZerega Estate on Ferry Point Park remained in the family from the 1850s to 1916. Their mansion, Island Hall, burned in 1895, and the smaller version shown here was built on the same spot.

Squire DiZerega (the name was later changed to Zerega) housed his thoroughbred mounts, Shetland ponies, and coach horses in this outsized stable apart from the farm animals.

Four

MERCHANTS

As late as 1968, this knife-grinder plied his trade in Middletown, Country Club, and Throggs Neck. Today, he would be followed by a horde of fascinated children, but back then he was taken for granted.

Joseph, Frank, and Nick Magazino stand in front of their Wonderfood Grocery store at 3186 Philip Avenue in this 1939 photograph. Loretta Borell became the next owner, and William Frobese acquired it in 1988.

The former Wissmann Carriage House in the rear survived this fire, but its cinderblock annex burned to the ground on February 10, 1953. It had been a paintspraying factory for typewriters and was located on Wissman Avenue.

This bill head is dated July 7, 1896, and is a reminder of the days when the Murphy family ran the grocery store that catered to the various estates dotting the area. The bill is made out to Mrs. B. Campbell, and her family ran a small farm on Miles Avenue for quite a while. Note the words in small print: Telephone Call, 19 Westchester.

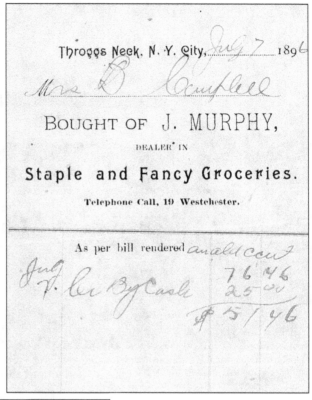

Throggs Neck, N. Y. City, *July 7* 189*6*

Mrs B Campbell

BOUGHT OF J. MURPHY,

DEALER IN

Staple and Fancy Groceries.

Telephone Call, 19 Westchester.

As per bill rendered

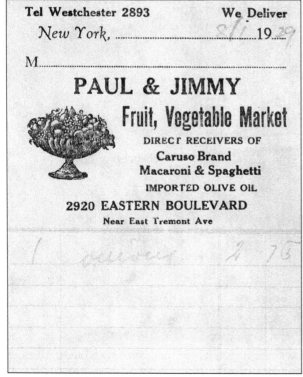

Tel Westchester 2893   We Deliver

New York, ... 19__

M...

PAUL & JIMMY

Fruit, Vegetable Market

DIRECT RECEIVERS OF

Caruso Brand
Macaroni & Spaghetti

IMPORTED OLIVE OIL

2920 EASTERN BOULEVARD

Near East Tremont Ave

This bill is dated August 1, 1929, and is from the Paul & Jimmy Fruit, Vegetable Market at 2920 Eastern Boulevard, near East Tremont Avenue. It was made out to Judge's Beach and once again, note the telephone number, Westchester 2893.

Tom's Villa Bianca Restaurant was located on East Tremont Avenue at Sullivan Place and was run very effectively by the Randazzo family until they decided to expand and open the Marina del Rey.

This picture of the Pelham Bake Shop was taken at their former location of 3048 Buhre Avenue. It was established in 1935 and has since moved to 1650 Crosby Avenue.

Catherine Converso provided this picture of Goonan's Bar on the south side of Bruckner Boulevard between East Tremont and Edison Avenues. The name of the bar was later changed to Flaherty's and then to Hurley's. From left to right are: Paulie (bartender), P. Stegmier, Ray Coulter, Al Ross, unknown, Tony "Chips" Tuccilli, Artie Gilmartin, Mickey Converso, two unknowns, and Bob Melville.

The Gate restaurant and dance hall on Harding Avenue, east of Meagher Avenue, owed its name to its location behind the gates of the Wissman Estate. Prohibition had just begun in 1918, so the place was regarded as a speakeasy. The sign at the right advertises Model tobacco.

Karl Fromwalt was the original proprietor of Charlie's Inn. He opened it as a restaurant on August 10, 1935, in the old coachhouse of the Morris Estate. The restaurant prospered from the very beginning and is now operated by the Gallagher family.

Karl "Charlie" Fromwalt operated this tavern as an adjunct of his restaurant, Charlie's Inn, at Harding and Balcom Avenues.

The P & P Builders Supply Company was started by the Pye and Paliotta families in 1927 at 242 Meagher Avenue, and their property extended east to Pennyfield Avenue. Six of their seven trucks are shown in this photograph taken at Meagher Avenue across the street from the swamps.

Various types of blocks were manufactured at the P & P plant including the tamped blocks shown here. Ford Pye Sr. poses upon the blocks with his dogs in this 1928 shot.

The name of the Ferris Brothers on the pharmacy window in this 1880 picture was the name of a family with roots in the Revolutionary past. The passenger was William Doherty who married May Ferris and who had a carriage shop on Zulette Avenue. The pharmacy was located in the village (now Westchester Square) and stayed in business until 1915 when Samuel Fritz took over for the next 45 years. The Ferris name was all over the maps of yesteryear. Ferris Point was an earlier version of Ferry Point, and a small port on Westchester Creek was Ferris Dock on Brush Avenue. Ferris mansions were on Rawlins Avenue, on Middletown Road, and an exact duplicate was located on Mayflower Avenue, and others were in and around the area.

Five

SPORTS

This 1929 photograph of the PS 12 baseball team was taken in Pelham Bay Park. Dr. John F. Condon, the principal, is in the center. He is recalled as the intermediary in the Lindbergh kidnapping case. Wesley Boes, who provided this picture, is in the front right.

Bill Zawar provided this photograph of the award-winning St. Frances de Chantal baseball team of the 1940s. His father, Louis "Doc" Zawar, was the trainer and is at left in the photograph.

Bill Zawar provided this photograph of the 1945–46 championship basketball team of St. Frances de Chantal. Msgr. William Jordan is seated front and center, and Louis "Doc" Zawar, the trainer, is standing at right. Note the errors in spelling on the banner.

William Linberg is seated at left, and Jim Geddis at right in this 1928 photograph of the St. Benedict basketball team. Only four of the five young men standing are identified, and they are Lester Marks, Bill Thiess, Jack Kearns, and Cornelius O'Brien.

Bocce is taken very seriously by the men in this photograph sporting their special tournament shirts. Somewhat akin to bowling, the sport came to the Bronx from Italy and is extremely popular in our area. It is also occasionally spelled bocci or boccie.

The Warriors football team, thanks to Jerry Demers, is among the largest sports attractions in the Pelham Bay area. The football players and the cheerleaders are known far and wide for their excellence.

Jerry Demers and Assemblyman John Dearie are pictured here at the Warriors award ceremonies.

Wesley Boes provided this 1934 photograph of the Wilcox Athletic & Social Club baseball team. Pictured, from left to right, are: (front row) Charlie Boise, Scotty Scumaci, and Peter Greco; (middle row) Larry Birsner, Bob Zawar, George Coulter, and Howard Milner; (back row) John Kerwin, Wesley Boes, Bob Maher, and Henry Fox.

Wesley Boes provided this picture of the 1934 Wilcox A & S Club basketball team taken after they claimed the championship trophy of the East Bronx Basketball League. Pictured, from left to right, are: (front row) Wesley Boes, Howie Milner, and Roy Hickey; (back row in uniform) Johnny Kirwin, Pete Greco, and Bob Maher. Tony Scumaci is to Bob's right.

The Ralph Giordano Funeral Home provided this picture of the Country Club team parading down Crosby Avenue. Note the Buhre Avenue El station in the background and Giordano's Funeral Home and Florist at left.

Vinaccia Field was located on the grounds of the Museum of the American Indian off Bruckner Boulevard and was the home field for the Pelham Bay Little League. The field was dedicated on July 26, 1970, in honor of Louis Vinaccia. Lou and Ernie's Pizzeria sponsored the team shown here.

The sign in the background of this picture indicates that the area is the "Future home of the Pelham Bay Little League." The Westchester Avenue El is in the background, and Tan Place is at the left. The name of this little street was later changed to Little League Place. The photograph was taken in June of 1982.

Mayor Ed Koch takes a swing at an incoming pitch with a shovel at the groundbreaking ceremony for the building at the Pelham Bay Little League Field off Tan Place on August 26, 1989. The Westchester Avenue El is in the background.

This photograph of the Lawton Aces was taken *c.* 1947. From left to right are: (kneeling) Mike O'Connor, Tom Wukich, Shorty Marziotta, Rich Gill, and Junior Cavaluzzi; (standing) Bob Kenny, Tony Ricci, Jimmy Kenny, Jim McLaughlin, John Harrington, Jerome Hussong, Joe Walsh, Joe Wukich, Rich Giampapa, and "Uncle" Art Marguard.

The Throggs Neck Little League 1965 All-Star Team included the men in the rear who are, from left to right: Adam Emhardt, John Morstatt, Freddie Ziehl, and Leo Vitti. The boys, from left to right are: (sitting) Al Stein, Robert Walker, John Albin, Joe Troiano, and Mike Frezza; (kneeling) Matty Pueraro, Rich "Corky" Derrico, Donald Ritchie, Larry Crosby, and Jeff Jonap; (standing in rear) Joe Bonaiuto, Danny Smith, Ray Bimbo, and Joe Zaffuto.

Construction of the Throggs Neck Little League headquarters on Throgs Neck Boulevard is proceeding in this photograph taken in the fall of 1971. Pictured, from left to right, are: (at ground level) John Hill, Harold Malkin, Richie Giampapa, Willie Speranza, Bob Jonap, and Ed Mooney.

Leo Vitti christens the new Throggs Neck Little League building on opening day in May 1972.

Gus Biebrich pitches a horseshoe in friendly competition at East 177th Street and Hatting Place. The sign at right in this 1949 picture indicates "Locust Point Civic Association, Inc.; playground and club house to be erected." The name of this section of East 177th Street has since been changed to Locust Point Drive.

Young men and women were allowed to have clubs in Edgewater Park, provided the clubs were separate and the members were 21 years of age. This group was called "The Bronx Rivals" and organized the first Edgewater Park Labor Day Games in 1919.

The Alinons were among the many popular baseball teams in the area, and this photograph was taken in 1928. From left to right are: (front row) Joe Iannuzzi, Gorizio Iannuzzi,and Joe Catucci; (second row) Walter Driscoll, Ed Vialonga, Pete Russo, and George Van Bomel; (third row) Al Iannuzzi and Dom Rotello; (back row) Joe Gelhaus, Frank Corelli, Paul Petersen, Oscar Straub, and the manager, Andy Strand. Joe Iannuzzi provided the photograph.

14 below zero
Feb. 9, 1934

City Island

Marco D'Antonio is pictured ice skating on Eastchester Bay near Singer's Beach in February of 1934.

Artie Treanor provided this picture of some of the Throggs Neck Clippers. It was taken c. 1950, and, from left to right, we see "Pop" Harry Nelson, Warren Krupp, Pat Daly, Larry Haskell, Brother Finn, and Dickie Nelson (boy).

The Old Colfords pose at Colford Oval at East Tremont Avenue and East 177th Street where Mandee's is currently located. Pictured, from left to right, are as follows: (front row, seated) Jackie Smith, Buddy McKenna, and Mickey Cunningham; (middle row) Jimmy Mongiello, Bill McGuigan (an umpire), Adam Natella, Tommy Patrick, and "Duke" Maragleno; (back row, standing) Tom Flynn, Bill Bressler, and manager Andy Cockburn.

This photograph of the New Colfords was taken in 1946. From left to right are: (seated) John Murphy, Sal Peninni, John "Dutch" Bresler, and Adam Natella; (kneeling) Harold "Ham" Abrahamson, Freddie della Salle, Manager Tommy Patrick, Bob Drabeck, John Werbowski, and Tom "Nin" Moore; (back row, standing) Paul Drabeck, George Frost, John Nelson, and "Gee" Lumina.

This representative picture of the A.F.C. Rapid Soccer Award Ceremonies at Wil Cintron Field on Balcom Avenue was taken on April 13, 1985. Members of the Raiders shown here, from left to right, are: (front row) Kenneth Bancker, Ed Laggenbauer, Anthony Pastore, Patrick Reid, and Billy Donohue; (back row) Coach Ed Laggenbauer, Bill Woods, Jimmy Lyons, Michael DeNiscia, Danny Landi, Chris Colombano, Steven Wade, and Assistant Coach Ken Bancker.

The soccer division of the German Sport Club of New York is captured in this 1945 photograph taken at German Stadium. Pictured here, from left to right, are: (front row, kneeling) Karl Koppel, Willie Ingwersen, and Franzman Scheeren; (back row) Eddie Trunk, Jimmy Hayes, Gerry Birkermaier, Richie Birgler, Otto Radditz, George Kaylor, Richie Giampapa, Joe Schnepf, Frank Rack, Bobby Schmidt, Linden Scheeren, and Joe Scheeren (manager). The photograph was provided by the Solfio family.

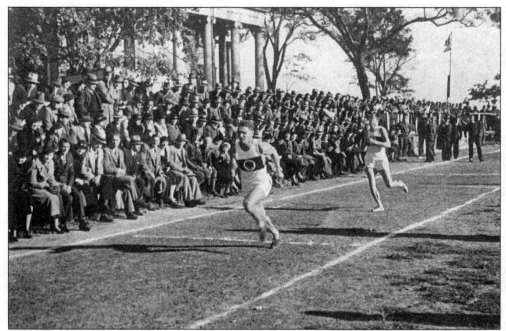

In this 1940 middle-distance race at German Stadium, Gene Zeumer, the stadium owner, won handily. The race was one of the many sporting events held there every weekend. In the immediate vicinity of the track were tennis courts, a soccer field, and a beach on the East River. The former Morris mansion is partly visible at left.

Tommy "Blackie" Muratore and Bobby Hearn are shown with their Hawks uniforms. They played on the field off Philip Avenue opposite the Lucarelli farm. John V. Riche, a former Hawk, supplied the picture.

Six

TRANSPORTATION

George Finnin Sr. provided this picture of two Oneida transport vehicles bearing 1922 license plates. The picture was taken at Diehl's Livery located at 3168 East Tremont Avenue, north of Waterbury Avenue.

George Finnin Sr. provided this photograph of Diehl's Livery located at 3168 East Tremont Avenue north of Waterbury Avenue. It was taken in the summer of 1912, and the sign on the building at center states, "coaches, landaus, stages and carriages to hire at all hours." Below that is the word "expressing." The small sign below that indicates "horses for sale." The trolley tracks in the foreground and the young man wearing knickers on the west side of the street next to the pole should bring back memories for the older generation.

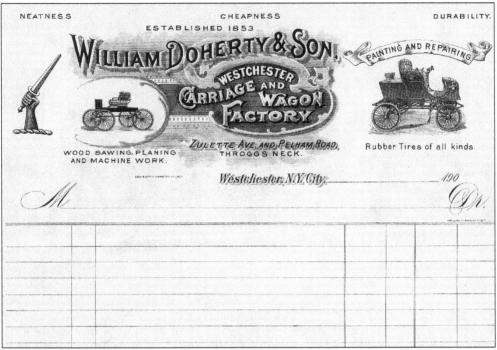

The Westchester Carriage and Wagon Factory was established by William Doherty at 2811 Zulette Avenue in 1853. He had been born in Coleraine, Ireland in 1825 and learned the business through an apprenticeship with his brother-in-law John Hatteridge. Doherty traveled first to England and then to New York City before establishing this business at Westchester Village.

This snapshot from George Finnin Sr. of the Silver Beach Camp bus was taken in July of 1921. The bus is fully loaded, and the driver even has a little boy on his lap, as they prepare for the trip to the car-line where they can board a trolley. That's a beanie the boy is wearing.

Some may recall the old stone wall in the background of this picture taken on Fort Schuyler Road (now Pennyfield Avenue), alongside Silver Beach. The driver is Mr. Klenck and the little boy next to him is his grandson, Fred Aram. Mrs. Aram, with the white collar, is in the rear.

The 1923 Jordan Play Boy pictured here was brand new when this photograph was taken. Fred Willing is behind the wheel and Mr. Shaw was the owner.

The first service station to open in Throggs Neck was Engeldrum's in 1924. Mrs. Engeldrum can be seen next to her gravity-fed Purol gasoline pump in this photograph. Her home is in the background, and the shop is at left.

This picture of Engeldrum's shows how it had grown over the years with multiple pumps. Note the Esso sign at the left and four signs offering Plaid Stamps in this scene from the 1960s. The gas station on East Tremont Avenue south of Lafayette Avenue has since been displaced by a Genovese store.

Bob Miller's 1923 Maxwell cab is parked at Tremont Avenue and Bruckner Boulevard. Note the Great Atlantic and Pacific Tea Company at left. Bob was one of the early entrepreneurs who carried passengers from the car-line to the beach clubs.

Ford Pye Jr. is still too young to work at the family business on Pennyfield Avenue, which served as the original home of P & P Builders Supply. The picture was taken in 1932, and a Pierce-Arrow delivery truck is behind the carriage.

This photograph of the Locust Point bus at East Tremont Avenue, north of Eastern Boulevard (now Bruckner), was taken c. 1923 and was provided by Kenneth Aitken. The bus is facing south, and the driver is Harold Aitken. Al Werner and Johnny Katsch are also in the picture. The Aitken family are among the pioneer families of Locust Point and once lived in the Wright Mansion.

The trolley car terminal at today's East Tremont Avenue and Bruckner Boulevard, looking north toward Westchester Square, was Schuylerville's prominent feature c. 1905. Tremont Avenue was then called Fort Schuyler Road, and Bruckner Boulevard was known as Eastern Boulevard. The photograph was supplied by Ronald Schliessman.

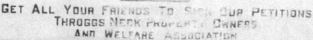

WE WANT ON TREMONT AVENUE
A CROSSTOWN SUBWAY LINE
FROM THROGGS NECK TO GEORGE WASHINGTON BRIDGE
GET ALL YOUR FRIENDS TO SIGN OUR PETITIONS
THROGGS NECK PROPERTY OWNERS
AND WELFARE ASSOCIATION

The sign in the background of this photograph reads, "WE WANT ON TREMONT AVENUE A CROSSTOWN SUBWAY LINE FROM THROGGS NECK TO GEORGE WASHINGTON BRIDGE—GET ALL YOUR FRIENDS TO SIGN OUR PETITIONS, THROGGS NECK PROPERTY OWNERS AND WELFARE ASSOCIATION." Below that, the area has been whited out so we can't tell what was there, but the upper background appears to show Helena Aram's building at the northeast corner of East Tremont Avenue and Scott Place, a building which once served as a draft board and later as a post office. From left to right are: (front row, seated) Mrs. Anna True, Mrs. Clara White, Mrs. George Hoffman, John F. Walsh, President John Moroney, Mrs. Charles Lipschultz, Frank Vogler, Mrs. Mary Heimbuch, and Mrs. Catherine Nelson; (back row, standing) Mrs. Mollie Palumbo, Mrs. Frieda Tooley, Mrs. Anne Georges, F. Juchster, Mrs. Catherine Vogler and Mary Catherine Vogler, Alderman James A. Deering, Mrs. Ruth Smith, Arthur Lipschultz, Mrs. Mae Deeks, Frank B. Vogler Jr., and Mrs. F. Juchster. The picture was taken c. 1925.

In the early years, no Throggs Neck community had public transportation but, rather, depended on jitney cabs that fanned out from trolley terminals. After WW I, private buses with solid tires had scheduled runs along bumpy roads to beach resorts and settlements.

A new traffic light in Throggs Neck was an occasion for celebration. This one was installed on the southwest corner of Tremont and Schley Avenues. Pictured from left to right are Jimmy Vacca, Peggy Vega, and Councilman Mike DeMarco, sharing the moment with traffic officials.

Casey, on horseback, was the Irish farmhand who worked for Richard Shaw during the early days of Edgewater Park. This photograph, taken c. 1918, shows the bungalows in the background, 9-A, 10-A and 5-A, and the Long Island Sound beyond the houses.

Jim McQuade, equestrian and proprietor of the Schuyler Hill Funeral Home, has donated horses to the Mounted Police Unit at Pelham Bay. In this scene, he is taking Councilman Michael DeMarco for a ride in Locust Point. The councilman, by the way, has since become a judge.

Seven

PUBLIC PLACES

The landfill mountain west of the Pelham Bridge was undreamed of when this shoreline was known as Tallapoosa Point. Since then, the cove and islands have been swallowed up and lost to future generations.

What is today's Weir Creek Bicentennial Veterans Memorial Park, facing the Long Island Sound, was once the 1915 pipeline construction over Weir Creek seen here in the foreground. Gravel and cinders were hauled in from Miles Avenue on narrow-gauge rails and spread by Italian workgangs.

Pictured running north at Schley Avenue was "The Sewer Road" A.K.A. "The Ash Road" or "The Cinder Path" that was overlaid in the late 1950s.

Julia Barnett Rice, M.D., had Rice Memorial Stadium built in honor of her deceased husband, Isaac L. Rice. The 5,000-seat bleachers were surrounded by a Greek temple, housing Louis St. Lannes' statue, *The American Boy*.

The Bronx County War Memorial was erected in Pelham Bay Park off the Bruckner Expressway in 1925. The 18-foot bronze Winged Victory was created by Belle Kinney and stands on a 75-foot-high column upon an 18-foot-high Vermont marble pedestal. The monument was designed by architect John J. Sheridan and dedicated to the men who died in WW I.

This second beacon stood on the west side of Fort Schuyler from 1826 until its demolition in 1944. "Captain" Charles Ferreira, seen here c. 1917, was the lighthouse keeper beginning in 1910. He had succeeded his father, Alexander, in the post.

This WW I cannon at Fort Schuyler was still protecting New York City from an invasion by sea when this picture was taken in 1942. The gun was facing northeast toward City Island. Earl Hansen took this photograph.

The Pelham Bay Library began opening on Saturdays in September of 1984, and Jimmy Vacca holds the ceremonial key to the facility in this photograph. The others celebrating the occasion are, from left to right: Joseph Licandro, Ann Hoffman, Kathy Williams, Lillian Lopez, Councilman Michael DeMarco, Vacca, Caesar Passadetti, Mike Crescenzo (kneeling), Vinny Tolentino, Assemblyman Eliot Engel, Phyllis Bufano, Angela Filomena, and Carol Holub.

A host of dignitaries, including the late State Senator John D. Calandra, came out for a parade celebrating the expansion of the Throggs Neck Volunteer Ambulance Corps to Pelham Bay. The April 13, 1985 parade started at the Pelham Bay train station and ended at Keane Square.

Split Rock in Pelham Bay Park was once surrounded by woods. When the Hutchinson River Parkway was planned, historian Dr. Kazimiroff rallied support to shift the road to spare the rock. Today, children still climb it.

Along Shore Road opposite Pelham Bay Park's Golf Course, an iron fence once guarded the Treaty Oak. There, Thomas Pell purchased the land from the Indians in 1654. The tree is gone, but a fence still marks the site at the entrance to the Bartow-Pell Mansion.

This picture of the giant cedar of Lebanon that once stood off the northeast corner of East Tremont and Schurz Avenues was taken on September 2, 1934. Planted by Philip Livingston *c.* 1790 it served as an aid to navigation until it came down in the hurricane of September 14, 1944.

Middletown lost a link to its Revolutionary past when the Spy Oak was cut down in 1933. It stood near Westchester and St. Theresa Avenues, and folklore persisted that colonists, spies, and soldiers were hanged on it.

The Civil Defense band traveled throughout the community during WW II seeking volunteers. The sign on the bus reads, "JOIN CIVIL DEFENSE, 45TH PRECINCT, 2877 BARKLEY AVENUE." The logo on the bus reads, "BOARD OF TRANSPORTATION OF THE CITY OF NEW YORK." The youngsters pictured are smiling broadly and apparently don't mind standing in the slush on this winter day.

Greta Zarookian provided this photograph of the unveiling of the WW II Honor Roll plaque on September 20, 1942 at the corner of Harding and Graff Avenue. It was donated by the Morris Estate Taxpayers Association, and Father O'Donald was on hand to bless it.

Westchester Creek separated Throggs Neck from the mainland, making the village (Westchester Square) a riverport for sailing vessels and barges. Today it is covered by the Lehman High School playing field. Ron Schliessman supplied this photograph.

Anthony R. Ferrara provided this picture of the WW II Honor Roll that graced the northeast corner of Crosby and LaSalle Avenues. It was erected in May of 1943 and was paid for by public subscription.

This photograph of the Bronx Whitestone Bridge under construction was taken in 1937. The bridge opened on April 29, 1939, in time for the New York World's Fair.

The Lawrence F. Keane Memorial on Westchester Avenue in Pelham Bay is a source of pride for the entire community.

Eight

WATER ACTIVITIES

Canoe tilting in the 1920s and 1930s was a popular contest around Labor Day. The long poles, padded by stuffed boxing gloves at the "attack" ends, kept the men unharmed but not dry!

Richard Shaw, owner of Edgewater Park, donated the lumber to anyone who volunteered to build a 30-foot tower in 10 feet of water. The skilled construction workers directed the "weekend carpenters," and the job was done c. 1927 off 15-B.

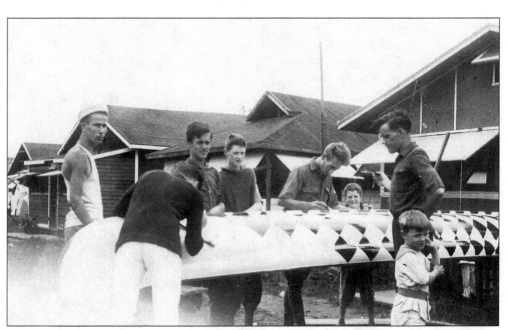

Painting designs on the canvas sides of wooden-framed canoes was a fine art in years past. Paul Miller provided this photograph from c. 1917. Milton Bennett, the artist, is at left, and the little boy is John McNamara.

Hunter Island was the site of a picnic celebrating the close of summer in this 1920s snapshot. About 30 people paddled up from Edgewater in six canoes and were towed home by the motorboat at the upper right skippered by Ed Greene.

Orchard Beach's development began in 1930 when barges brought in enough sand to fill in Pelham Bay itself (middle right) and also to create the parking lot off to the right. City Island is seen on the left.

Schuyler Hill, a small community between Pennyfield Avenue and Hammond's Cove, enjoys a view of the distant Throgs Neck Bridge. The prominent Locust Point Yacht Club (center) now covers a once popular sandbar that was located here when the cove was called the lagoon.

Askov Hall was established as a meeting place for the Trinity Danish Young People Society in 1920. They soon relocated to their current location at Dean Avenue on the Long Island Sound.

The Silver Beach waterfront is alive with activity in this photograph from the 1920s. Beyond the pole at the end of the wharf is a float buoyed by two pontoons. Several rowboats are moored at left, and a couple of others are on the beach.

Silver Beach in the mid-1920s showed little change from the 19th-century estate of the Havemeyer family. The tide is low, and the wharf is on the left. Two young men, one a lifeguard, are standing next to the rowboat on the right.

Annual swimming events are held by the White Cross, Manhem, D.A., Turner, and Askov Hall clubs, as well as by Silver Beach and Edgewater Park.

Inter-club aquatic contests along the Throggs Neck shoreline are a century-old tradition. The D.A. Beach Club's initials on the clubhouse signify "Deutsch-Amerikanischer Klub," a phrase which probably needs no translation.

This photograph of John Smyth, a son of the caretaker of the DiZerega Estate, was taken next to the dock on Westchester Creek in 1908 at Ferry Point.

The Orchard Beach Chapter of the Coney Island Polar Bear Club posed for this picture during one of their annual winter frolics in the Long Island Sound.

German Stadium Beach was run by the Zeumer family when this picture was taken off Schurz Avenue. Bathers stopped at Solfio's Refreshment Stand on their way to the beach, which was occasionally "invaded" by kayakers who camped overnight in tents near the mansion. The mansion is seen in the background, where songfests were held deep into the night.

Off Wissman Avenue there is a breakwater that was built of granite blocks in the 1890s. A 20-foot upright iron pipe supporting a barrel warns shipping during high tides. Summer campers in 1920 rest there at low tide.

Squire Wissmann had a pole and barrel above water at the end of his jetty to alert mariners, but, in a dense fog, a fishing boat did strand itself. All that day, in 1919, it hung until high tide returned.

Most residents of the east Bronx will recall Bronx Beach and Pool. Located at Longstreet Avenue and East 177th Street, it opened c. 1929 and attracted a steady stream of bathers for decades. It offered both the salt water of Long Island Sound and a huge pool and always seemed to have a special of the week, such as a "most freckles" contest, twin days, or red head days. Diving and swimming exhibitions and competitions, bathing beauty contests, and singing contests were held, and dance bands were brought in for evening entertainment. There was a picnic area, handball courts, a cafeteria, and plenty of free parking. Ron Schliessman provided this photograph.

Nine

PEOPLE AND PLACES

The Lorillard Spencer Estate, at 129 acres, was one of the largest to be incorporated into Pelham Bay Park. It is from this estate that the Spencer Estate Civic Association draws its name and the name for the community sandwiched between the park on the north and Country Club on the south.

On the Fourth of July in 1942, the Edgewater Park All-Girls Band was formed by families whose mothers were active on the home front as their fathers were away at war. Not having instruments, they marched in many parades singing patriotic songs and became well known. Later, the girls learned to play instruments, and boys were admitted. This later photograph shows, from left to right: (kneeling) Joshua Flood, Erin Finnegan, Michele Falzon, Christine Schellenberger, and Kristian Flood; (standing) Cele Mutze, George "Pepe" Peragine, Dorothea Geffken, Paul Mutze, John Mullane, John Falzon, Paula Mutze, John Peragine, Patrick Petriello, Eddie and Jamie Schellenberger, Eugene Balasenowich, Nancy Lacerra, and Theresa Peragine.

The Silver Beach Board of Directors, led by Eugene Connelly, met with city and state officials on April 18, 1987 to discuss the reassessment of the co-op. The officials present are State Senator Guy Velella (second from left), followed by Councilman Michael DeMarco, Borough President Freddie Ferrer, and Tax Commissioner Rod McKeon.

The North Bronx-Westchester Neighborhood Restoration Association donated $2,500 to the Adult Day Healthy Care Program at Providence Rest Nursing Home. From left to right are Sister Joanne Marruso, Dr. Vincent Squilla, and State Senator Guy Velella.

Frank Morea provided this interesting picture of 825 Calhoun Avenue. The view is toward the Whitestone Bridge, which can be seen dimly in the background. Note Philip Avenue and the Luccarelli farm at left.

Margherita Luccarelli was born in Ottaviano, near Naples, in 1897 and moved to Throggs Neck with her husband in 1921 where they established their farm on 73 acres. Her husband died five years later, and Margherita raised her eight children alone on her farm, which ran from Revere to Quincy Avenue on the south side of Philip Avenue. There was also a potato patch on the north side of Philip. Margherita is remembered with fondness by her neighbors and customers.

Weir Creek Bicentennial Veterans Memorial Park is shown in this picture taken after an annual Veterans Day Parade. From left to right are: Tom Hansen, Congressman Mario Biaggi, Jimmy Vacca, State Senator John D. Calandra, and Vinny Tolentino.

The "bookmobile" is parked at a scheduled stop on Dewey Avenue at Edison Avenue in this 1950 photograph. PS 72 would be at right, and the signs on the vehicle read, "The New York Public Library, Extension Division, Bronx Traveling Library."

John V. Riche provided this photograph of his wife, Margaret, in front of their home on Lawton Avenue. The white water tank with the three stars indicates that three men are active in the armed services. The sign at the right is a "For Sale" notice by Realtor Wilfred Reeder.

In 1924, the summer bungalow colonists in Edgewater Park lost no time readying their own volunteer firefighters. The men hauled this wagon, learned fire regulations, and even had a "boys' brigade." The little mascot on the front seat, next to Chief Donohue, is Freddie Aram.

This 1910 view of East Tremont Avenue and Eastern (Bruckner) Boulevard shows two features of the era: horse manure and the cost of refreshments. Note that a frankfurter on roll, an ice cream soda, and a frappe are all priced at 5¢ each, as was Coca-Cola.

The 45th Precinct Community Council presented awards to Donald Engledrum and Rose Johnson at their meeting of October 19, 1983. From left to right are: Mary Salemi, treasurer; Fran Mahoney, representing Assemblyman John Dearie; Lillian Schneeberg, vice president; Marge Jeffries, president; Engledrum, Johnson, and Dolores Baez, representing Borough President Stanley Simon.

Linden Avenue in Silver Beach already had a substantial number of houses. The view in this photograph is northward, looking toward the present-day Little League field. The bicycles of the 1930s, shown here, were "one-speeders."

Silver Beach homes did not evolve from tents as other settlements did. Catalpa Place, shown here, led north to open fields and some popular berry patches.

This is a 1918 view of Harmony Lane, Silver Beach's summertime colony that is now covered by St. Frances de Chantal School on Harding Avenue. The tents faced east to what later became the Little League ballfield.

Ron Schliessman took this photograph at the unveiling of the veterans' monument at DeRosa-O'Boyle Square. The memorial was made possible through the efforts of Tony Scumaci and John V. Riche who had it erected with the assistance of Mike Menna of the United Veterans Day Parade Committee and with financial assistance through LECET. Bill Twomey, shown here, was the Master of Ceremonies for the dedication.

Angelo Mastrarrigo is the subject of this 1946 photograph taken on East Tremont Avenue, south of Dewey Avenue. The taxpayers across the street were razed when the approach to the Throgs Neck Bridge was built. The former Migel Place would be to the right of the buildings.

The Bruckner Expressway had not as yet been trenched through, and, thus, there is no Tremont Avenue overpass in this 1965 picture. The photographer, Ron Schliessman, was looking north toward Westchester Square when he snapped this picture on March 1 of that year. An astute eye may catch the Coca-Cola advertisement at the extreme upper right showing that the company was still using that corner to promote their product.

Ten

SOCIAL ACTIVITIES

Led by Donald Braithwaite in March of 1921, the Unionport Walking Club used Split Rock Road across Pelham Bay Park from Boston Road to the Shore Road. Today, the lane is confined to the golf course.

The "Giglio" has been proudly carried along Waters Place in recent years, and, prior to that, Ericson Place was the center of the Bronx celebration.

State Senator Guy Velella is at left in this "Giglio" scene, and the popular Mario Biaggi is to his right. The latter had served as congressman for the area for many years.

The St. Frances de Chantal Sea Cadet Corps Annual Retreat of the 1967–68 season is portrayed here. John V. Riche (second from right) was the commander and Frank Twomey Sr. (at left) was the executive officer.

Elsie Thomma provided this picture, taken in the late 1940s, of St. Benedict's Fife and Drum Corps.

H. Westerman provided this 1944 photograph of the Silver Beach Band, which features, from left to right: (front row) Harold Parnham, majorette Joan Smith, Commander Ernest Stead, and Michael McGrory; (second row) John Fanning, John Gerhard, Kathleen McGrory, Arlene Maglietta, Audrey Garrison, Jack Becker, Carl Bauer, and Donald Perkins; (third row) Lee Denahan, Norma Blum, Mary Reedy, Beradine Hayes, Estelle Dwan, Doris Nowell, and Walter Denahan; (top row) Jim O'Reilly, Jack Schmidt, Michael McCabe Jr., Ethel Lavoie, Jane Jackson, Jeanne Palmer, Ruth Krupp, Laurel Kempf, and Miriam Greiss. The Hammond Mansion, also known as the Silver Beach Mansion, is in the background.

The Waterbury/LaSalle Community Association was founded in September of 1979 by Tony and Evie Ferrara. This photograph was taken a few years later, and among the political leaders shown are Councilman Mike DeMarco, Assemblyman John Dearie, Congressman Mario Biaggi, Jimmy Vacca from CB 10, and State Senator John D. Calandra.

When this photograph was taken on June 9, 1941, Harding Avenue ended at Baxter's Creek instead of Ferry Point Park as it does today. This converted barge catered to fishermen and boaters in the daytime and drinkers and dancers at night. The barge had the first juke box on "the Neck."

The Annual Throggs Neck Halloween Parade was started by State Assemblyman John Dearie and continued by Steve Kaufman when he was elected to the state assembly. This photograph was taken at the southwest corner of Miles and Tremont Avenues.

The social hall at left served as a silent movie house, roller skating rink, dance hall, basketball court, and bingo hall in Edgewater Park. This 1930 scene also shows the shopping center that housed about 15 stores.

In 1915, Irish immigrant Richard Shaw leased an estate on Eastchester Bay in order to run a horse farm. Coming from Mott Haven, he invited his church's St. Ann's Cadets to bivouac there. Parents later camped on the farm on weekends, and Edgewater was born.

Frank Lisanti took this picture of his daughter, May, in 1936 in front of 511 Revere Avenue. Note the open lots to Tremont Avenue and PS 72 in the left background.

Until his untimely death, Mike Menna had been running the Veterans Day Parade from Lafayette and Tremont Avenues to Weir Creek Bicentennial Veterans Memorial Park. The Grand Marshalls for 1989 were Nick Florio (WW II), Victor Anderson (Korea), and Philip Cremins (Vietnam).

This photograph of Lou Swift was taken on the DiZerega Estate in 1908. He is exercising a greyhound belonging to Mr. Price, a cotton broker who was renting the adjoining estate of Pierre Lorillard.

Among the activities of the Siwanoy was snaring fish on a receding tide. Although reeds were generally used, the stone enclosure pictured here is thought by some to be an Indian weir. The photo, provided by Wilma Turnbull, was taken at Palmer Cove.

As far back as the Revolutionary War, this was Pennyfield Lane, but, in 1888, it was designated as Meagher Avenue to honor the famous Civil War general. John and Betty McNamara posed in 1916 with Harding Avenue behind them as the photographer looked south.

Italo Mazzella provided this picture of a walking tour that included Schuylerville. The view is to the southeast, down Haskin Street, and Bill Twomey (with microphone) and John McNamara (second from left) led the group.

A strolling scene photographed on Silver Beach in 1936 was taken of Edgewaterites, who are identified as, from left to right: Mary and Pauline Ungerer, Arthur Schwarz, Mary Howard, Bob Rossbach, and "Penny," the dog.

"Watching the Labor Day Games" marked the end of each summer in Edgewater Park. The two boys at lower left in this 1920 picture are the McNamara brothers.

The summer of 1920 in Edgewater Park closed with a masquerade parade and party for the children.

The annual Halloween pumpkin sale of the St. Frances de Chantal Catholic Youth Organization is recalled in this October 1984 photograph taken at the entrance to the rectory driveway on Hollywood Avenue. From left to right are: Sylvia Tennel, Gerard DiPreta, George Marino, Mario DiPreta, and William Donovan. Father Ed Barry was the group's director.

The Silver Beach American Legion Post holds "Pearl Harbor Remembrance Day" ceremonies annually at the Redwood Club on Schurz Avenue. Following a parade to mark the occasion, Edwin Lamond, who was stationed at Pearl Harbor on December 7, 1941, tossed a floral wreath upon the waters.

128

Printed in the USA
CPSIA information can be obtained
at www.ICGtesting.com
LVHW071025211223
766685LV00056B/925

9 781531 600099